Grow the tastiest and most nutritious food

Nature's Way

Practical guide to making excellent soil and producing excellent food for hobbyists, gardeners, communities and enterprise growers

Ronald Gilchrist   Alfred Grand   Marion Jess

This book is a joint project between Greenway Consulting in the west of Scotland and VERMIGRAND, the Organic Biohumus company in Lower Austria.

Dedication

This book is dedicated to the unsung heroes, the farmers and gardeners everywhere who work tirelessly to grow tasty and nutritious Organic food for their families and neighbours.

Authors

Ronald Gilchrist BSc, MSc, MIBiol, ACIWM, FLS is an ecologist with experience in farming, education and environmental research. He heads up Greenway Consulting Scotland, a not-for-profit Community Interest Company specializing in training. He is a specialist in domestic and commercial composting systems. His recent research has been into vermiculture and community food production. Ron is an inspirational speaker and accredited trainer in these fields.

Alfred Grand is an expert in soil fertility. He is an Organic farmer in Lower Austria. In 1999 he set up his company, VERMIGRAND, solely for worm composting. Its main activity at present is the production and sale of their Organic certificated mineral enriched VermiGrand Biohumus. Alfred has a special interest in education and community Organic food production. In cooperation with universities, his research currently is in developing different activated compost teas for special applications like horticulture, turf management, agriculture and vineyards.

Marion Jess, part of the Greenway team, after many years in education, has in recent times concentrated on growing produce sustainably and eating as freshly as possible. Much of the produce shown in this book was grown in her own garden or in her community garden raised beds. Marion edited the content of the book and played a major role in its design.

with additional input from . . .

Jade Peters, our Greenway chef who has such a passion for freshness, flavour and nutrition.

Angus Starling FRIAS

ANGUS DESIGN
Illustrations

Acknowledgements

We acknowledge the support of the Scottish Government through the Climate Challenge Fund and Social Entrepreneur programmes.

Our thanks to all the gardeners at our Fairlie, Bothwell and Forres Community Gardens in Scotland and to the teams at The Education Park, Die Garten Tulln, and at Natur im Garten[Nature in the Garden]Office, Austria who have done so much to support and encourage us as we develop the Green-way gardening method.

In Scotland, thanks to . . .

Sam Jess at Greenway who developed the HotBox

Sandy Niellands of Fairlie for his constant support with wormcast production

Bill Gow who project managed the Bothwell garden

Avril Clark and May Gow who are such passionate propagators

Brisbane and Kelburn Primary Schools, Largs

Michaela Hunter of Community Woodlands Association Scotland

Donald John Campbell of Sabhal Mor Ostaig College, Isle of Skye

Last but not least Scott McGregor of Largs Printing Company who so patiently and cheerfully worked on the page layouts for this book.

In Austria, thanks to . . .

Alfred's wife Marion, who constantly encourages him and provides tasty and healthy food from their organic garden for Alfred and everyone at the farm. Also thanks to his partner in VERMIGRAND Leopold Fischer, who takes on a lot of the work and so makes it possible for Alfred to have some time for research, development and going forward in the right direction.

PUBLISHED BY GREENWAY CONSULTING (SCOTLAND) CIC.

PRINTED IN SCOTLAND BY LARGS PRINTING COMPANY.

First Edition   © 2011 by Greenway Consulting (Scotland) CIC. All rights reserved.

Contents

Introduction

Easy by Design – which model suits you 1
Space considerations 2
Time considerations 3
Who will use your garden 4
Hassle free gardening 5
Windowsill model 6
Patio/Driveway/African model 7
Courtyard garden model 8
Community Garden model 9

Wormbox – making excellent wormcast 11
Building a Wormbox 13
Type of worms 15
Living conditions 17
How to feed 21
Harvesting wormcast 22
Storing and using wormcast 24
Winterising your Wormbox 25
Wormbox FAQs 26

HotBox - making excellent compost 27
The Process 29
Building a HotBox 31
Recipe for success 33
Feedstock Mix 34
Particle Size, Moisture, Temperature 35
Maturing and using your compost 37
Winterising your Hotbox 39

Developing Excellent Soil Fertility 41
Soil Composition 43
6 Steps to excellent soil fertility 45

Excellent Produce - grown intensively 49
Maximising food production 51
- horticultural hints from the potting shed

Growing for Health 57
Fresh is best! 58
Scrumptious Salads 59
Soups 60
Sauces and herbs 61
Abundance 62

Localise 63
Excellent food is affordable 64
Localise to recession-proof your community 65
Localised thinking and enterprise 66

Look deep into Nature and then you will understand everything better.

Einstein

Introduction

The way our food is currently produced is heavily dependent on fossil fuels and their derivative chemicals. As the cost of oil increases, **the cost of our food will continue to spiral.**

"A Farm for the Future", Rebecca Hosking's revealing BBC documentary [available on YouTube], highlighted how serious this is for our future.

We have to find a more sustainable way to produce our food.

This book describes just such a way – the Green-way.

By learning from Nature and developing permaculture principles, with the minimum of materials, anyone – anywhere – can build a Grow Your Own (GYO) garden and grow food.

Currently in our global village there are over **94 million people in food poverty** – their community may have food but they cannot afford to buy enough to feed their families.

This book details your steps to . . .

- design and build your own garden

- maximise your soil fertility

- grow gardens full of delicious and nutritious herbs, salads, fruits and vegetables

- save money and eat healthy food

- create a sustainable community garden

This Hands-on Guide will allow you to **recycle your kitchen scraps and garden waste** into top quality **FOOD** - lots of it - **without using chemicals.**

Regardless of skills, abilities and how much space you have - **anyone can do it** – the Green-way.

Earthworms are the
intestines of the earth

Aristotle

Easy by Design

Grow your own food - the Green-way

Everyone has different needs and resources, so even the best design for one person will not be the best for another. But if you get the design of your garden right for you, growing excellent vegetables is easy the Green-way.

There are **THREE** key considerations ...

- **What SPACE do you have?**

- Traditional allotments work very well for some but many people cannot acquire one OR one may be more than they can cope with because of its size or their fitness to make it work OR because of the amount of time required.

  Using the Green-way, with ...

  - a few pots on your windowsill
  - a few planters
  - a raised bed in your garden
  - a community garden

  anyone can grow significant amounts of food.

This is essentially "container" gardening.

These "container" gardens can be built on urban gap sites, contaminated land, in the corner of a playground or even on your balcony, patio or driveway.

- **What TIME do you have?**

- For people with limited available time, more food can be produced per square metre in a small bed with excellent soil fertility than in larger plots.

   Fertile soil allows greatly reduced spacing between your plants. This reduces moisture loss from the soil but, most importantly, it also greatly reduces the opportunity for weeds to grow.

   Even during the summer months, if you keep a layer of mulch between your rows of plants, very few weeds will appear.

   Not only does this save your valuable time, but weeds reduce the amount you will grow each year by stealing precious water and nutrients from your soil.

   More plants = less space for weeds

   Less weeding = saved time, and time freed to sit in the peace of your garden and relax!

Islay Community Garden, Scotland

Fairlie Community Garden, Scotland

- **WHO will use your garden?**

- By using raised beds 600mm high, the soil is easily reached and so can be kept with a good consistency by occasionally forking it over with a hand fork.

  When available time is limited, the smaller the growing unit, the more attention the soil and the plants get.

  There is good access for everyone – for wheelchair users, for people with weak backs and for children, the beds should be no more than 900mm wide so that any part of the soil can be reached from the side of the bed. For more able gardeners, the bed should be 1200mm wide.

  NEVER stand on the soil – so there will be no compaction and …

  - weeds are easy to pull out
  - the soil has lots of air spaces
  - soil drains freely
  - it will heat up early in the Spring
  - even during wet weather in wintertime, you can easily work the soil.

Brussel sprouts need to have soil compacted round their roots

All the tools needed by a Raised Bed gardener

Hassle-free gardening

With clean dry paths between the beds, wide enough for a wheelbarrow or wheelchair, there is no need to haul on big boots every time you want some herbs or a salad - indeed, you can garden in your slippers if you really want!

The paths between the beds should be as narrow as possible and should be covered with weed-suppressing membrane. This can be covered with gravel or wood chip for visual impact.

No digging! In our fertile woodlands, the soil does not get dug or ploughed so, if you learn from Nature, it is not necessary to dig your growing area either.

In the woodland soil, there is a good population of earthworms which pull leaf fragments down from the surface and mix the soil layers.

By keeping a thick layer of mulch on your beds, especially during the winter months, lots of earthworms will be attracted to your bed and they will do the digging for you.

By springtime your soil will be full of nutrients and plant growth substances.

Excellent soil conditions yield lots of excellent vegetables – the key to healthy families.

Which model suits you?

Growing lots of your own tasty and nutritious herbs, salads, fruit and vegetables can be easy and require little time, if …

- you design your garden with small, accessible units
- you get into the habit of using Organic methods to maintain excellent soil fertility

Windowsill herb garden model

Fresh and delicious herbs can make an ordinary meal special – basil for a pasta dish or a parsley sauce with fish. You do not need handfuls of herbs. A **small amount** is all that is required. Even if all you have room for is half a dozen herb pots, that is enough.

- Use as big pots as you can - they are less prone to drying out
- Always use the best Organic soil mixture [see page 44]
- Regular watering is essential
- Each month sprinkle a little biohumus [see page 46] round each plant, rake it and water it in.
- Get into the Organic habit. **Any use of chemicals** will reduce the soil fertility and compromise on the amount, and the quality, of your herbs.

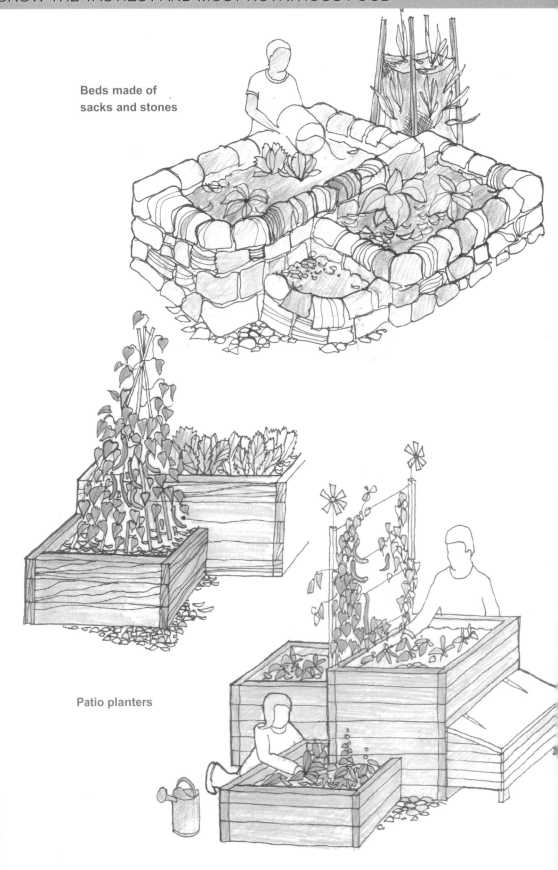

Beds made of
sacks and stones

Patio planters

Courtyard garden model

If you only have small area available to you, then the **three dimensional model** should be considered…. copying Nature.

In a woodland, light is trapped first by the tree canopy, then by the shrub layer and finally by the ground level plants

Copying this model …

- we grow planter or cordon **edible trees** [apples, pears, cherries, figs, cobnuts].
- under these we have **edible shrubs** [blueberry, raspberry, loganberry, boysenberry, tayberry and quince [on the north-facing side].
- if we plant **in the ground** under these, the tree and shrub roots will take most of the moisture and nutrients. Instead **lay down weed-suppressing membrane** first to exclude these roots [and any pernicious weeds], and place your raised bed(s) on that.

You will have three layers to harvest. **Easy!**

Community garden model

This is a great place to **make friends** and **exchange ideas**. It will be a **social hub**, **outdoor gym** and **peaceful nature reserve**.

This can be a community project where everyone works together to produce food for the community – as with the Islay Community Garden [photo page 3]

If individual beds are required, design in a range of planters, small and large beds, plots and, if soil is not contaminated, you can also incorporate plots and community orchards with fruit bushes and trees.

Rather than everyone having their own shed, you may consider having a community shed like the Fairlie Garden, incorporating a meeting room, a tool store and an open shelter area where members can meet and put the kettle on.

You may replicate the Bothwell Garden and also have photovoltaic electricity generating panels on the roof. With an import/export meter, it will earn money during the summer. This will more than pay for any light and heat you may need for your propagator units during the winter. **Easy!**

Before

After

Best design for me?

What space I need . . .   Windowsill ? Driveway ?

What I can really grow . . . salads, herbs, onions . . .

What I need to start . . . the right size of "containe

Think!   pots?   boxes?   beds?

Grow   - what I would like to eat

       - what suits my climate

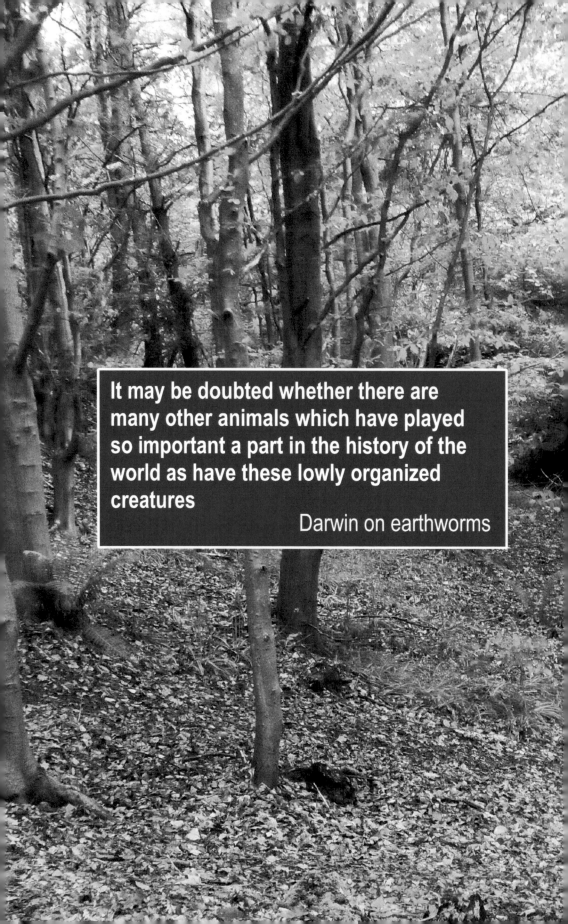

It may be doubted whether there are many other animals which have played so important a part in the history of the world as have these lowly organized creatures

Darwin on earthworms

WormBox

Make and Use your own
WormBox - the Green-way

Animals which are particularly important in breaking down organic matter in woodlands and reducing it back into its component nutrients are the worms.   There are many kinds of worms but we are interested in the litter worms which live near the surface of the forest floor.   Learning from Nature, we can harness the same process to create fertile garden soil by farming these worms.

This is called **Vermiculture**.

With this process, your kitchen scraps and garden waste can be converted into a supply of the exceptionally potent plant and soil tonic, **wormcast biohumus**… and it's FREE!

It's called biohumus because it is the organic soil component called humus but it is teeming with an extraordinary diversity and number of beneficial soil microbes.

Just a trace of this in your soil and your plant vigour will be exceptional.

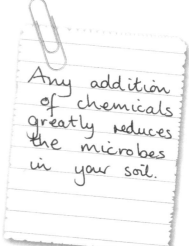

Any addition of chemicals greatly reduces the microbes in your soil.

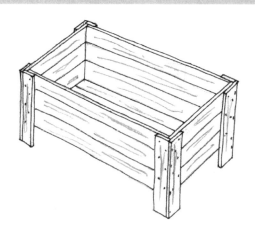

Building a WormBox

Build it with **WOOD**. In the sustainable organic garden we try not to use fossil fuel or its derivatives… so, avoid using plastics. Anyway, in cold weather, condensation forms inside plastic wormeries, creates lots of moisture and this can flood the box. Worms prefer to lie against a wooden surface … and THICK wood serves as winter insulation for them.

Composting worms are surface dwellers and so the ideal WormBox has a large surface area and a small depth. No breathing holes are needed in the sides, if the box is made of wood, as the worm bed breathes through the top surface.

The Domestic WormBox

900mm long x 500mm wide x 400mm deep [in school box shown the legs lift the box 100mm off the ground]

Properly looked after, this box will process all the kitchen scraps from a large family.

With an insulation layer inside your box the worms will remain fully active all winter and by the start of the growing season, you will have a copious supply of free organic fertiliser.

If your WormBox has **legs** and is located on sharp gravel, it should keep your worms safe from attack by the predatory New Zealand flatworm which is common in many areas.

Make a **lid** for your box. It need not be water-tight but should fit well enough to keep out voles and shrews looking for a cosy home for the winter – especially one teeming with their favourite food – worms!

For a community garden or school or college, a **Playground WormBox** should be 1200mm long x 600mm wide x 500mm deep.   There is so much biological activity in every quarter of a square metre, it has been found that boxes bigger than this are less productive area for area.

Your Wormbox can be located next to a north facing wall – it doesn't benefit from the warmth of the sun.

Earthworms

In any soil, it's important to have a big population of the deep burrowing earthworms. Some come to the surface like Lumbricus terrestris, others live deeper in the soil. They are "Nature's plough", mixing the different layers of soil, helping the soil to drain and letting air into the plants' root zone.

However, these earthworms have a very slow metabolism – they don't eat much - and so are not the best composting worms.

Litter Worms

Composting worms [also known as brandling or tiger worms] are the species found just under the surface in our woodlands. They have a fast metabolism, can eat up to half their own body weight of food per day and are responsible for quickly breaking down the autumn leaves, converting them into **wormcast biohumus**, the fertiliser for the next season.

These worms can be found in farm manure heaps but there are species and varieties which are specially good for composting because of their great appetite and breeding rate.

Different species perform differently and prefer different conditions.

Types of litter worms

Eisenia fetida, the redworm, prefers warmer conditions - it has a huge appetite and has the best breeding rate.

Eisenia hortensis, the bluenose, is a bigger, tougher worm - does well in a wider variety of conditions, is a very reliable worker, but does not breed as quickly laying less eggs in each capsule.

Eisenia andrei and *Dendrobaena veneta* are smaller than the bluenose but have a similar performance.

Worm Breeding

Worms are hermaphrodite – every individual produces young. They can mate every 2 weeks and shortly after, lay their egg capsule.

The capsule is lemon shaped and about 1.5mm long. It starts lime green and turns brown as it gets ready to hatch – this takes about 2 weeks. Six to eight weeks later each of their offspring will start to breed!

This is why a healthy wormstock can double in size every 3 or 4 months.

Loads of Worms…

If the bed is getting over-populated, the adults will produce less young and then start to leave the box to find a new eco-space to populate.

It is good practice to divide your worm bed two or three times a year so that you always have young [hungry] worms working for you. This is your chance to start someone else with a WormBox.

If you do not split your stock, some worms will simply leave the box and find your compost heap to live in or populate your garden.

How many investments do this?

It's a win-win situation!

16

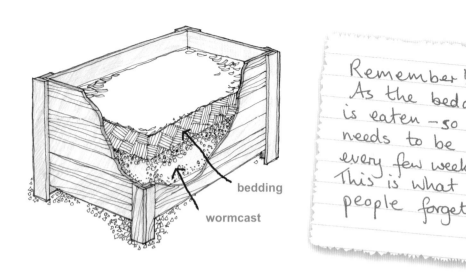

bedding

wormcast

Remember!
As the bedding is eaten – so more needs to be added every few weeks. This is what most people forget!

To start a Domestic WormBox, buy 1 kg of worm - this may be about 1,000 worms.

Getting your worms to work well for you is like looking after any pet – give them the living conditions they need, water, their favourite food and they will thrive.

These "litter worms" are found among the leaf litter in our woodlands – a moist, fibrous environment.

The conditions in your box must copy this.

Living Conditions 1

Bedding

The bedding layer is where they live and feed. It must be fibrous, moist and containing lots of air spaces.

To start a new wormbox, put a layer of semi-rotted compost on the floor of the wormbox.

On top of this goes the bedding for the worms – 150mm of moist, fibrous material – copying the conditions of the forest floor.

Worms do not have lungs. They breathe through their skin which must be kept moist or they will suffocate. Make sure the bedding never dries out.

Their metabolism is so rapid that they need plenty of air. The bedding layer must be moist but, if it contains too much water, it will become waterlogged, and the air spaces will be flooded.

Choosing Bedding Materials

The materials you use for bedding will depend on the season:

Always cover the top of the bedding with some coarse brown cardboard or paper.
This keeps the surface moist and this is where the worms come when looking for romance!

Good Materials

- semi-rotted compost from your compost heap
- brown, fibrous corrugated cardboard [e.g. egg boxes-torn up and made moist]
- soft leaves - not waxy or glossy [bag up lots in the autumn and store behind the shed to keep you supplied all winter]
- horse, sheep or rabbit bedding
- horse manure
- some grass cuttings - not too many as they may heat up quickly and worms don't like to be cooked!

Inferior Materials

- Paper [contains lots of clay and little wood fibre]
- glossy cardboard
- glossy leaves like beech or rhododendron

Getting the moisture right!

To keep the moisture level just right, do the Squeeze Test. When you squeeze a handful of bedding in your hand, only a couple of drops of water should appear. This will give the worms exactly the conditions they prefer and they will work hard for you.

Their new home is ready for habitation.

Doing the Squeeze test regularly will ensure that your wormcast will remain aerobic and sweet smelling – just like the lovely smell of the leaf litter under trees.

Beware!

- the lower layer of a WormBox should **NEVER** be waterlogged! Waterlogged means **NO AIR**:

- anaerobic bacteria are all that will survive and they are not beneficial!

- wormcast will become sour and smelly as hydrogen sulphide, sulphur dioxide and methane gas are given off.

- a WormBox should **NEVER** have liquid draining from it. This liquid will contain some nutrients but is the sign of poor worm husbandry.

You should be able to!-

Put your head in the Box!
Inhale deeply!
Smell the sweet smell of leaf litter under trees.

Bedding too dry? -
sprinkle some water from your watering can and do squeeze test.

Bedding too wet? -
tear up some cardboard and mix it with the bedding

Living Conditions 2

Food

Worms are always hungry!

They need a regular supply of moist kitchen / catering scraps as their food.

Keep a clean "caddy" with a lid under your sink and put your peelings and scraps into it.

Good Feedstock Materials

- Fruit & vegetable peelings
- Eggshells - crushed
- Coffee grounds (with filter paper)
- Tea bags
- Pasta
- Rice
- Potatoes
- Brown cardboard

Note Not much onion, garlic or citrus fruit – it gives them indigestion!

Ideally the kitchen scraps should be chopped up as finely as possible, particularly tough skins or stalks.

The worms will also eat the bedding as it breaks down and becomes soft.

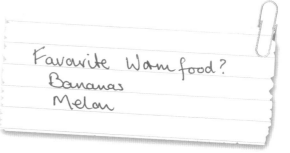

Favourite Worm food?
Bananas
Melon

How to feed

Feed at least once a week :

- Make a trench in your bedding
- Spread the scraps from your kitchen caddy along the trench
- **Cover it over** [worms prefer to work under the surface and it will avoid attracting fruit flies]
- Put a marker where you have fed and when you come to feed again, dig the next trench slightly along from the first trench. This way the bed will be evenly fed over a period of time.

If you are going away for 2 - 3 weeks, double the thickness of your bedding layer. Make sure it is moist. Your worms will graze on it while you are away.

The worms are very active and so will quickly find the food wherever it is.

If you maintain a 150mm layer of bedding, your worm population will grow according to how much food you give. If you do not have a lot, the population will remain small.

Worms do not have teeth.

They essentially feed on soft material. However, like poultry, they do have a muscular sack in their digestive system, the **gizzard**, where food is ground up. For this their digestion is speeded up by sprinkling a handful of sand or rockdust [see page 47] onto the bed every month or so.

How do I harvest my wormcast?

As the worms climb upwards towards the "restaurant" and eat their way through the bedding and food, they will leave behind the precious **wormcast biohumus**.

The amount of wormcast you produce will depend on your husbandry skills, the quality of your bedding and how many kitchen scraps you have.

If you keep your worms working all year, your WormBox may fill up three times each year.

With experience, a WormBox 1300 x 600 x 500mm can produce 1 tonne / 1300 litres of lovely rich, mineral enriched wormcast each year!

This would normally be used as a mix with ordinary compost.

When the worms are living near the top of your wormbox - **that is the time to harvest!**
To bring them into the top layers, spoil them with a fruit smoothie! They will definitely come up for that.

> Weekly tasks:-
> - Do the Squeeze Test
> - Loosen the bedding to make sure they have sufficient air
>   Warning! only loosen the bedding. DON'T disturb the wormcast
> - Feed your scraps - chopped up finely!

Community and commercial wormcast production

The Six Steps

Removing the wormcast is a very easy and quick job.

1. Get yourself large buckets or other containers.

2. Lift off the bedding layer and put it into a bucket. You will have removed most of the worms with it - any left in the lower wormcast layer will be good for your garden when you spread your harvest.

3. You will recognise when you have reached the wormcast layer. The wormcast is a black, heavy, sticky, material - not fibrous.

4. Dig out the wormcast from the bottom of your box and store it in a suitable container [watertight and covered] in a cool place.

5. Place a layer of fresh bedding in the bottom of the WormBox and put the worms back into their box. Feed them and make sure the bed is moist enough.

6. Cover them up.

Job done!

Wormcast   Bedding

Storing your Wormcast

Ideally, harvest your wormcast during the spring and summer when you are ready to use it − it is at its most biologically active when it comes out of your WormBox.

However when you become so good at looking after your box that during the winter it is full and MUST be harvested − the best place to store it is in a wooden box.

Do not sieve the wormcast − just store it.

Cover the wormcast with cardboard and carpet or bubblewrap and spray its surface with water every month until you are ready to use it.

If the wormcast is stored in a plastic bin condensation can cause it to go anaerobic

or

If the wormcast is stored in a breathable sack it may dry out……

In either case, its potency will decline rapidly.

Using your wormcast

- Mix the wormcast with 10 x the volume of ordinary compost and some rockdust [see page 47] and use this premier compost mix to top dress your garden soil at the start of the growing season
- Add very little to your seed compost. Seeds do not need many nutrients
- Sprinkle some of your wormcast/compost mix into the planting holes when plantlets are being planted out in their final position
- Sprinkle round your house plants, rake into the surface soil and water lightly
- Mix 50ml biohumus with dechlorinated water and use as a soil drench

Winterising your Wormbox

If you want your worms to keep producing wormcast throughout the winter – you should aim to keep the bedding in your Wormbox at a temperature >10°C.

To ensure this – some hints…

- Line your box – some insulation will help keep the worms from freezing up. Polystyrene 50mm thick will last through one winter. However it is easily damaged and can become waterlogged, so you may want to protect it with plywood. OR To make an insulation lining which will last for the life of your box, treat yourself to plastazote. It is very tough, has similar thermal insulation properties to polystyrene and no plywood protective lining is required.

- Plan to harvest your wormcast biohumus so that your box is more than half full as you go in to winter.

- Make sure that you keep your bedding layer >150mm thick. [leaves, horse manure]

- Keep trenching lots of peelings and food scraps into your bed. This will decompose, generating some heat.

- If there is a body of air above your wormbed in the Box, this will be cold and will draw heat out of the bed. Cover your bed with layers of bubblewrap, pieces of carpet or other insulation. Also mid-winter, fill the top half of your box completely with dry leaves. This will trap air and act as a duvet, keeping your workers warm in the coldest conditions.

With an air temperature of -15°C and a strong windchill, with experience, you should be able to keep your bed at 10 - 15°C!

If there is lots of snow – pile it up around your Wormbox. It will keep the cold wind off and act like an igloo.
At least your worms will be warm!

FREQUENTLY ASKED QUESTIONS

- **WormBox does not smell sweetly?**
- Your box is too wet. Leave the lid off on a dry day. Take the cardboard / paper cover off your bed. Loosen up the bedding and leave to dry in the wind. Tear up some brown cardboard and mix it with the bedding layer. Cover up again before night.

- **There is a mass of tiny white worms in my bedding?**
- You have overfed your worms. The kitchen scraps in some of the bedding have become too acidic. The little worms are called Enchytraeids. They are good friends of the worm farmer and act as an indicator species. They too are composting worms and there always will be some in your bedding layer. When there is a mass of them, it is an indication that you should loosen up your bedding and not put any more feed in for at least a week. They will soon disperse.

- **There are woodlice in my WormBox?**
- This is not a problem. They are decomposers too.

- **There are ants in my WormBox?**
- Your bedding is too dry. Ants need a dry place to set up their nest. Keep your bedding a bit too wet for a week. The ants will soon pick up their eggs and move on.

- **There are tiny flies around the Box?**
- These are fruit flies. You have not buried your feeding deeply enough or covered it over with bedding.

Wormbox notes

Date	Observation	Action
12 August	Fruit flies!! Bedding too wet	bury food deeper mix in cardboar

Date	Observation	Action

If one way be better than another, that you may be sure is nature's way.

Aristotle

Excellent Compost

Make excellent compost the Green-way

Microbes make biohumus. – the key to the fertility of our woodland soil

Composting is an aerobic process [meaning air must be present at all times] in which microbes break down organic wastes. This converts your food scraps and garden wastes into a supply of a lovely, sweet smelling, brown powdery material – compost!

Composting is **microbe farming** – give the microbes their favourite living conditions and they will work constantly for you – making lots of biohumus to enrich your soil.

Humus - the key to soil fertility in Nature.

Once the decomposing microbes have done their work, the composting process is complete and the compost can be stored without the need to let more air in.

An excellent compost . . . does not contain any weed seeds or pathogens.

An excellent Composter . . . is someone who is able to process their organic wastes and produce excellent compost **throughout the year**.

The Composting Process

Composting involves the activity of billions of naturally occurring microbes which are aerobic - like the worms and like ourselves, they need air.

If we have no air, we will die. The aerobic microbes are just the same. They will die. A composter is a microbe farmer! If you give them the living conditions they need, water and their favourite food and they will thrive .. and work hard for you.

In your compost pile in the absence of air, another type of microbe takes over - the anaerobic microbes. They do not make good compost.

If your compost bin is a bit smelly, it is too wet and has become anaerobic. The smell is due to the release of gases like sulphur dioxide and hydrogen sulphide which are toxic to plants [and to us!] but methane gas [one of the main contributors to global warming] may also be released.

To become an excellent Composter, there are two different stages in the composting process which must be managed:

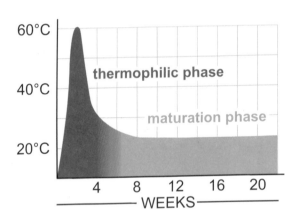

Stage 1:
Thermophilic [hot] Process

It has to be **HOT!**

You may have noticed that if your cut grass is moist and you gather it in a bag and leave it to one side, it will heat up. This is caused by special, naturally occurring microbes multiplying rapidly as they feed on the grass cuttings.

Such is the intensity of the microbial activity that the biomass may heat up until it is too hot to touch. The heat indicates the great intensity of the metabolism of these heat loving microbes and results in three things:

- the organics will breakdown very quickly
- all the weeds and weed seeds will be killed off
- any pathogens [diseases] present will also be killed off [sanitised]

This stage takes only two or three weeks if you use a HotBox.

Stage 2:
Maturation Process

This is a COLD stage.

This process is a long chain of reactions - in a certain sequence and involves very many different species of microbe -

the breakdown product from one organism becoming the feed for the next.

Since it is a chain of reactions, it cannot be speeded up.

It takes 4 or even 6 months for the breakdown of the organic material to be complete. After that, your compost is biologically stable – it no longer needs to be turned to let more air into it.

Many people find that it takes one or two years before their waste has completely broken down … and even then it contains weed seeds. This is because they have omitted the most important **FAST** theromophilic stage.

If they process their green waste in a HotBox first and then put it into their usual compost container, then these problems will be solved

This simple Hotbox is neatly under the trees with a traditional plastic compost bin for maturation.

There are so many microbes - naturally in your garden wastes - that there's no need for an "accelerator" to innoculate your heap

Building a HotBox

Many people complain that their compost bin smells or that it attracts flies and that garden waste takes a couple of years to break down.

They are disappointed in the quality of their compost and it still contains weed seeds.

The cause is that they have omitted the **thermophilic [HOT] composting phase** – any heat that is generated when they put their grass cuttings into their bin is lost through the plastic walls.

The solution is simple. Make yourself a Box which is insulated on all 6 sides and cannot lose heat. Then **ALL** the heat which the microbes generate will be retained in the pile. The thermophilic microbes will thrive in such numbers that your green waste will break down very quickly.

You make yourself a wooden HotBox to make sure that:

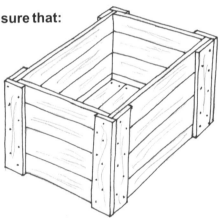

- the initial short, hot thermophilic phase is successful,

- the biomass has reached 55 – 60°C.

- all pernicious weeds are killed

- all weed seeds are killed

- all pathogens [disease causing organisms] are killed

After trying various materials, we have found that having an insulated wooden box is the best solution.

In sustainable gardening, wherever possible, we avoid the use of fossil fuel or its derivatives.

The Domestic HotBox composting unit –500mm x 500mm x 500mm

It must be thoroughly insulated on all six sides.

It must be **totally** sealed so that no heat can escape.

Then it is possible for your batch to go from ambient temperature to >60°c in just 36 hours!

This size of Box ensures that, if the mixture has the right composition, there is enough material in it to reliably heat up quickly.

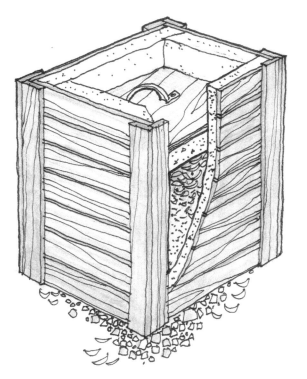

However, this is a batch process.

You cannot just put material in every few days. Gather your garden materials (a garden waste reception bay, as pictured below, would be ideal) until you have enough to fill the Box.

The Box needs to be filled, the lid put on and then left to complete the 14 day cycle.

The smaller the biomass in your compost heap, the more difficult it is to reach your target of 55° – 60°C.

Once you are confident that you have got the recipe right, you can try making a smaller HotBox which has just the right capacity for the amount of garden waste you generate each fortnight.

Visit us online . . .

www.green-way.org.uk

Our online community is growing. Be a part of it!

The Hotbox Batch Recipe for Success

Equipment you will need:

- Your HotBox
- Chopping box
- Thermometer
- Garden fork

Factors for successful composting -

- feedstock material mix
- particle size
- moisture content
- temperature

This is a BATCH process.
Collect enough material to
completely fill your Box.
You shouldn't add more
material once the process
has started.

The HotBox Batch Recipe for Success

Feedstock Mix

For your HotBox a mix of 60:40 green:brown material can be used, contrary to traditional practices.

Green material
- grass cuttings
- weeds
- fresh leaves
- vegetable peelings
- fruit peelings

Brown material
- cardboard [not glossy]
- sawdust
- dry leaves
- hedge clippings
- wood chip

The green material contains the nitrogen required by the microbes and generates the heat in the mixture.

The brown material contributes the carbon they need and, most importantly, the coarse, woody material gives a good structure to the mix – trapping lots of air.

Particle size

The smaller the particle size of your material, the quicker the waste will break down.

Therefore to speed up the process chop up or shred all bulkier material in particular the brown material -- hedge clippings, small branches, etc.

However, it is good to have some twigs present to form air spaces in the pile. These may still be present at the end of the process but they can just be sieved out and added to the next batch

Moisture content

Microbes are only active in **moist conditions – not wet.**

Make sure - mix the components of the recipe well so that the whole heap is moist, but not wet.

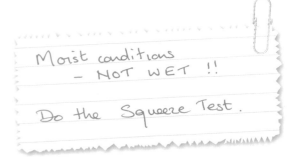

Moist conditions
– NOT WET !!

Do the Squeeze Test.

If it contains too much water, the air spaces will become flooded and the aerobic microbes will suffocate.

Then fill up your Box, tightly fit the lid and **watch the temperate soar!**

Temperature

To ensure that all your weeds and any pathogens have been destroyed during the 2 week cycle, the material in your HotBox should **reach 55 - 60°C for at least 3 days.**

A small thermometer – such as you get for an aquarium is a good way of tracking the rise in temperature.

Check the temperature daily – watch it rise!

Towards the end of the first week, the temperature will start to drop as the microbes use up all the air. The mix should be **forked or lifted** out of your box, loosened up and returned to the box.

Your pile will have reduced a lot in volume already!

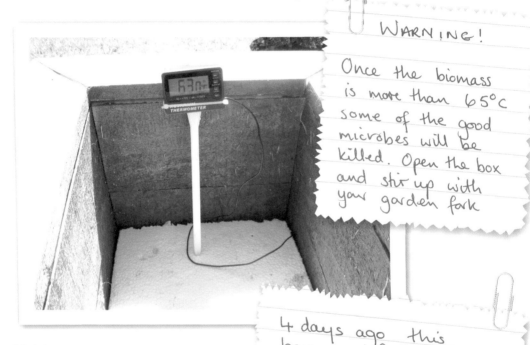

WARNING!

Once the biomass is more than 65°C some of the good microbes will be killed. Open the box and stir up with your garden fork

4 days ago this box was full to the top! Reduction in volume is more than 50%!

Moisture may have evaporated off, so you may need to **sprinkle some water** onto the pile. Then seal up the lid again for a further week. During this time, you should have 55°C again for another 3 days.

After two weeks:

- the mix will have **reduced in volume** by 50 – 70%
- have a soft, moist consistency
- temperature will have started to drop again.

The most important fast **thermophilic phase** of the composting process has been completed!

Stage 2 : Maturing your compost

This semi-composted material from your HotBox will have reduced a lot in volume and the weed seeds and any diseased material will have been sanitised … but it is not yet **mature compost.**

Now you have two options:

Either **use it for bedding** for your WormBox. It is soft and juicy and so the worms can eat it quickly and produce lots of biohumus. Note that the longer the material is in the composting process, the less food value it has for the worms – cool it down and get it into your WormBox immediately after the 14day thermophilic cycle.

OR

Make it into **a mature compost** - Stage 2 of the Composting process.

For this cold maturing process, fork the semi-composted material from your HotBox into a wooden compost box or plastic compost bin.

Keep your compost covered at all times:

- to retain its moisture
- to prevent weed seeds blowing onto it

Maturation will take 4 – 6 months.

Fork over the top layer of your maturation pile **every month** as there will still be some microbial activity needing air.

If the pile starts to smell sour, it has become anaerobic. It may be too moist or may just need to be thoroughly forked over.

When mature, if the Compost you have made is a friable, moist, sweet smelling material which does not generate weeds, **you have succeeded in making excellent Compost.**

CONGRATULATIONS NOW YOU ARE A COMPOSTER.

Using your Compost

Whenever you dig your Compost into your garden, you are locking carbon into the soil humus, **the soil carbon sink**. Instead of the carbon being released into the atmosphere, it is deposited where Nature intended – incorporated into the humus content of our soils.

This is a very effective response to the challenge of Climate Change.

The more herbs and vegetables, and even more importantly, the more bushes and trees you grow in your garden, the more carbon is being locked away - the greater your contribution to greenhouse gas emission reduction.

The more Compost you incorporate into the soil, the greater will be your soil fertility [see page 45] and the resulting productivity of your garden.

If you sieve your Compost:

The finer material should be put:

- into your potting mix
- into the holes when you are planting out your plantlets in the garden.
- onto the soil around your pot plants, raked and watered in.

Add 10% wormcast biohumus and some rockdust to your fines to make your own blend - **excellent compost**

The coarser material should be

- dug in around all your shrubs and trees each year
- dug into all your flower borders and vegetable beds when you are top dressing them in the Spring.
- Mixed with basaltic rockdust and wormcast biohumus to really "turbo charge" your soil! [see page 46]
- Kept as a layer of mulch on top of your soil throughout the year [see page 48]

Bothwell propogators

**Winterising your Hotbox -
keep it generating mulch
throughout the winter**

Many people only use their HotBox during the summer when they have a regular supply of fresh grass cuttings and hedge clippings.

They aim to store enough bedding during the summer to supply their WormBox throughout the winter.

The HotBox can be lovingly stored away until next Spring.

Some real composting enthusiasts like the challenge of keeping their HotBox working all year round. To do this, find a source of fresh horse, cow or sheep manure to use as an alternative to grass in your HotBox feedstock recipe. This, mixed with your autumn leaves and torn up waste cardboard, if suitably moistened, will heat up well. See the steam rising from the uncovered HotBox.

In winter a 3 week process cycle works well with the biomass being turned over each weekend to introduce more air into the system.

Wormboxes and
Hot Box in
winter snow

Winterising your garden soil

If you do not need the product for Wormbox bedding, layer it onto your garden as a **mulch**.

In Nature, the woodland soil is covered in leaf litter during the winter.

Benefit like mother Nature.

- Soil insulated in the coldest weather
- Soil prevented from drying out. Microbes and litter worms cannot survive when the soil is dry
- Soil attractive to earthworms which will plough your soil for you.

The mulch feeds the soil food web – the millions of microbes in the soil. The decomposing organic matter continues to generate lots of nutrients and plant growth substances for the next growing season.

I deally you should aim never to have bare soil in your vegetable bed.

Hotbox notes

Start date	Batch Mixture	DAY	1	2	3	4	5	6	7	8	9	10	11	12	13	14
		Daily Temperature °C														
12 August	grass, cardboard sawdust, hedge cuttings		18	41	58	62	64	59	55	59	63	65	65	61	57	55

turn mixture let in air

80% volume reduction

Accuse not Nature: she hath done her part; Do thou but thine.

John Milton

Soil Fertility

Restore Excellent Soil Fertility the Green-way

Historically, farmers alternated growing a crop in a field with using it as pasture for their sheep and cows. The animal manure deposited humus back into the soil.

However, for many decades now, it has become the practice on many farms each year to remove crops from our fields and only replace the nitrogen, phosphate and potash in chemical fertilizers.

Here's Nature's secret revealed !

What Nature has done successfully for millions of years is surely worth copying.

Nature has fertilised our woodlands and kept them growing profusely year after year without human intervention.

If we can learn its secret, we can restore the fertility of our soils and we can imitate the prolific growth of a natural woodland.

Soil is composed of :

- a mineral component
  this came down with glaciation

- an organic spongy component
  *called **HUMUS** comes from the breakdown of dead plants and animals.*

- air

- water

- the soil's inhabitants
  bacteria, fungi, protozoans, springtails, worms

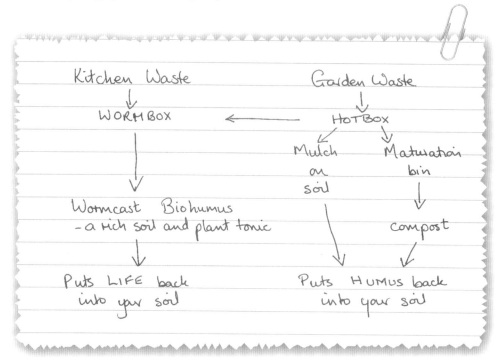

Kitchen Waste   Garden Waste

WORMBOX ← HOTBOX

Mulch on soil   Maturation bin

Wormcast   Biohumus
— a rich soil and plant tonic   compost

Puts LIFE back into your soil   Puts HUMUS back into your soil

Twin HotBox + WormBox unit

Quality soil = quality plants

To return fertility to our soil the humus and all the other elements in the crops have to be replaced.

We can do this:

- by digging in lots of quality compost to replace the humus
- by applying basaltic rockdust to replace the missing trace minerals
- by the application of wormcast biohumus to put the life back into tired soils

44

The Six Steps to Excellent Soil Fertility

With these SIX key steps you will restore and maintain excellent fertility in your soil.

STEP 1.   Apply Compost

Nature recycles **every bit of organic debris** that falls to the ground and converts it into soil humus.

Using our HotBox and WormBox system, you can do the same.

This system concentrates all the nutrients from the kitchen and garden waste into the rich, concentrated soil and plant tonic, **wormcast biohumus**.

This puts **life as well as humus back** into our soils.

If a soil lacks

humus:

- It will not be able to retain much moisture – a major issue during periods of drought
- Water will run off the land when it rains heavily – washing away soil nutrients and causing flash flooding
- It will not be able to support much of the soil life – bacteria, fungi, springtails or worms – on which plants depend for the efficient uptake of minerals into their root cells.

Lack of humus in our soil and the constant application of chemicals to soil destroys much of the microbial life in the soil – for example - the beneficial bacteria, fungi, protozoans, springtails, worms, etc – which enable plants to take nutrients into roots.

STEP 2.   Apply Wormcast Biohumus

Wormcast Biohumus is produced by worms and is a humus which is **teeming with beneficial microbes**. The numbers and biodiversity in every cubic centimetre of wormcast is so enormous that it is almost incalculable.

Applying **even a trace** of this biohumus to your soil has a dramatic effect on your plants. It puts life back into soils but also contains many enzymes and plant growth substances.

It is in effect a potent soil and plant tonic.

Our kitchen and garden organics are too valuable to throw out.
We should try to recycle every scrap and get it returned to the soil.

To find out more about soils we recommend 'Teaming with Microbes'

Teaming
with
Microbes
The Organic Gardener's Guide
to the Soil Food Web
REVISED EDITION

Jeff Lowenfels & Wayne Lewis
Foreword by Elaine Ingham

Die Garten Tulln

STEP 3.
Incorporate SEER Basaltic Rockdust

Our food can lack many **essential trace elements**, for example we need **selenium** to help us avoid cancer and **molybdenum** to help our energy levels.

In Nature trace elements entered the soil during glaciation.

Rather than wait for the next ice age to bring glacial deposits to your soil!

Replace the trace elements by using basalt rockdust.

This is not a quick fix. Over weeks and months it releases the minerals into your soil. This increases microbial activity and biodiversity – including nitrogen–fixing bacteria. It also improves the ability of soil to absorb and utilise CO2 [carbon sequestration].

STEP 4.
Only apply ORGANIC soil additives

Whenever we eat food which has pesticide residues, colouring, flavouring enhancing or other chemical additives – it can reduce our health and vitality.

The scraps from this food will contaminate the biohumus we produce and reduce the number and variety of the soil life it contains.

If there is an infestation of pests, seek a biological control method – like a nematode for slugs and companion planting for carrot fly [see page 53].

To build MAXIMUM NUTRITIONAL VALUE into what you grow and eat – incorporate basaltic rockdust in 3 ways:

① Spread some over soil whenever you topdress veg. beds

② Mix some into the batch each time you fill your HotBox

③ Spread some on top of your Wormbox each month

Fresh organic vegetables smell and taste wonderful!
You can save so much money by growing your own – and eat healthier!

STEP 5.
Only use DECHLORINATED water

Chlorine is added to our drinking water to kill off any microbes that may be in it.

Because of this, try **NOT** to use mains water directly on your garden.

Use rainwater if possible or always allow water to sit in your water butt or watering can **overnight before** using it.

This allows any chlorine to be released.

STEP 6.
Keep the soil covered in mulch

- Reduces the need for watering. It will slow down water loss from the soil – especially during periods of warm and windy weather.

- When a soil dries out, the microbes it contains will be killed. Nature always has a layer of leaves or leaf mould covering the soil.

- Mulch is a food source to keep your underground army of microbes fed – especially during the winter when there will be less plant debris falling onto the ground.

- Mulch will break down to add extra humus to your soil

With these 6 steps you will regenerate the poorest of soils, your plants will be very strong and you will enjoy the most delicious and nutritious meals.

Feeding your soil

Area Fed	Date			
	Compost	Biohumus	Mulch	Rockdus
Vegetable Beds (all)			5ᵗʰ October	5ᵗʰ Octob
Veg beds (all)	24ᵗʰ March	24ᵗʰ March	24ᵗʰ March	24ᵗʰ Mo

Area Fed	Date			
	Compost	Biohumus	Mulch	Rockdust

Earth is here so kind, that just
tickle her with a hoe and she laughs
with a harvest. Douglas William Jerrold

Excellent Produce

Grown intensively the Green-way

You can have an abundant supply of the most succulent and delicious herbs, salads, fruit and vegetables.

Once you have done the following . . .

- designed and built your vegetable garden to suite your own lifestyle and to make the best use of the available space
- got soil into your beds which drains well at the lower levels by incorporating sand and grit
- have excellent fertility in the surface layers by adopting purely organic methods
- incorporate basaltic rockdust to ensure that your produce contains all the essential trace elements you and your family need to be really healthy

. . . **then** you will be able to grow a **remarkable amount** of food.

Photo opposite - Alfred lifts his veg at Die Garten Tulln.

It will have an exceptional **flavour**. It will save you **money**.

You will know that your family are getting the very best nutrition.

Maximising food production

What else can be done to improve your crop?

Top tips from our potting shed

1. **Good quality compost**

   When you are buying compost for your seed trays and for your pots, always treat yourself to the best you can find – organic of course.

   You are investing so much of your time and energy into getting your garden to produce, and into developing a vigorous soil food chain biodiversity, it is not an "economy" to buy cheap compost which may contain any number of chemical contaminants.

2. **Organise your potting shed**

   Make things easy - have soil, sand, compost, rockdust and wormcast biohumus all to hand.

   Take time to mix up the ideal compost mixture for your seed trays, your potting on, planting out or for top dressing your vegetable beds.

Remember! Your seed compost should have very few nutrients.

3. Use a cloche

Incorporate lots of humus into your soil so that it will be able to hold lots of water and so be more drought tolerant.

However, if there is a prolonged period of dry, warm and windy weather, the condition of your young seedlings may still deteriorate.   By placing a cloche over them at this time it stops the plants being stressed and creates lovely still humid conditions for rapid growth.

4. Plant more closely together

With the rich nutrient soil you have made you can plant more closely together than normally recommended. There is food for all in the soil!

By close planting there is less room for weeds and it will reduce evaporation from the soil surface.

5. Attract insects

A colourful flower display will help to attract insects to your plot – among them the bees which will fertilise your fruit trees, berry bushes, tomatoes, etc.

Just as ladybirds eat greenfly [aphids], having a diverse insect population in your garden will greatly reduce the chance of other insect infestations. Lacewings and hover fly larvae devour aphids and white fly.

Make an **insect hotel** for your garden to provide accommodation for the many different predators which will help to protect your crops.

6. Companion and sacrificial planting

Choose carefully what crops you will sow next to one another. If you plant alternate rows of carrots and onions, the smell of the onions keep the carrot fly away.

Plant some marigold plants among your vegetables. Marigolds exude substances from their roots and leaves which repel pests such as white fly and so protect the neighbouring crops.

Slugs prefer marigolds to lettuces so plant a row of the big American or African ones – they will be more effective than the smaller French and English types.

Also plant some nasturtiums through your vegetable plot. Aphids prefer their leaves to lettuce leaves.

7. Keep disease pathogens out!

Using wormcast biohumus helps to keep many disease pathogens out of your soil. Earthworms and the composting litterworms only eat dead and decaying material.

You will often find them in the root ball of your plants – not eating the roots themselves but eating the microbes living next to the roots. Sugary exudates released by the roots attract the microbes.

They then deposit their microbe packed biohumus right next to the roots.

Worms have been shown to actively seek out and devour many pathogenic [disease causing] microbes such as E. coli and Salmonella. The fancy name for this is the **vermi-stabilisation of pathogens**.

When you add worm biohumus to your soil, many plant and animal pathogens will disappear. With a fertile soil having dirty hands is not a health hazard.

Community polytunnel, Fairlie.

Sabhal Mor Ostaig College, Isle of Skye.
All the veg were grown in the box shown.

8. Predator attacks!

Wildlife is wonderful and adds so much interest to our gardens but it has to be managed - sometimes it is "them or us".

Get smart – devise your own devious strategies to make sure that they do not win the battle!

Caterpillars and carrot fly

- This rapid growth in your garden will produce particularly succulent leaves – the perfect place for butterflies to lay their eggs, knowing that their offspring will be eating only the very best!

  It can be infuriating to watch your little carrots dying off as their roots are being chewed up by **carrot fly**. Time to mount a counter-attack!

- Try erecting a cloche over your bed [see page 52]. Bend lengths of flexible plumbing pipe to form hoops over your vegetable bed. Cover with a fleece like enviromesh. Then every plant will be safe from attack, you will maximise your crop… and you can **RELAX!**

Slugs and snails

- They can be a pest, particularly in soils containing a lot of humus and organic materials. Do not use slug pellets which will kill a wide range of your soil biodiversity and birds and mammals.

- Make a beer trap by pouring a little beer into a small tub, sinking it in the soil and covering it with a piece of slate. The slugs will be attracted to it, climb into the beer and die happy!

- Metal overhang round the bed stops slug invasion as in this photo from Die Garten Tulln.

- For particularly precious plants, cut the top and the bottom off a plastic drinks bottle and place the collar round individual plants

- Once plants become more mature and so more fibrous and tougher, they are less prone to slug attack.

9. Nature's Counter Attack

What happens in nature?

- **Blackbirds** and **thrushes** are good at collecting slugs and caterpillars for their hungry young. **Blue tits** are particularly fond of greenfly but **robins** and **sparrows** also eat insects.

- If you have a wood pile in a quiet corner of the garden, a **hedgehog** may take up residence. It will love tracking down any tasty slugs and snails.

- If you have room for a marsh area, **frogs** and **toads** will also patrol your garden at night for their favourite food - slugs .

- Online you can buy some **nematodes** which specifically infect soil molluscs. It comes as a powder. Mix it with water [dechlorinated or rainwater] and water it over all your vegetable beds and planters. The slugs which will soon disappear. This treatment should be applied three times during the summer.

- Slugs don't like sharp surfaces. Spreading crushed egg shells, sharp gravel or sand around your delicate seedlings [or surrounding them with copper wire] deters them.

Produce notes

Date	Harvest
13 August	loads of parsley - wash, cut, freeze
17 August	courgettes - cook with garlic + freeze
"	apples (fell from trees) make into purée
	loads of salad leaves - purée + freeze for :

Date	Fruit / Vegetables

Treat the earth well. It is not given to you by your parents. It was loaned to you by your children.

Ancient Native American Indian Proverb

Growing for Health

The fruits of your hard work - Enjoy

When your ingredients are of an exceptional quality, sometimes the less you do the better!

The fresher your ingredients and the less cooking - the more nutrients your food will have retained.

Here are some ...

- favourites from our kitchen
- hints for herbs and
- ideas for excess produce.

Scrumptious Salads

NEW POTATO AND HERB SALAD

- 1kg of new potatoes
- bunch of garlic chives
- small bunch each of: flat leaved parsley, mint, coriander, basil [or your own preferred herbs] all finely chopped
- zest and juice of 2 lemons
- 100ml crème fraiche
- salt and roughly cracked black pepper

At the ready have a pot of steadily boiling salted water and a bowl half full of cold water, topped up with ice.

It's very important when cooking new potatoes to have your pot of well salted water up to a steady rolling boil. When you put your potatoes carefully into the water the nutrients will be sealed under the skin. (putting potatoes into cold water and slowly warming them up will cook out their goodness).

If the potatoes are soft when pierced with a sharp knife, pour them into a strainer and then quickly into your bowl of ice and water.

In a large bowl mix the crème fraiche with your boiled potatoes, add the herbs and season to taste.

SPINACH SALAD

- 4 handfuls of baby spinach
- 1 pear sliced
- 1 handful of toasted walnuts
- 50g of shavings of your favourite hard cheese (parmesan, pecorino)
- 1 handful of seedless white grapes halved
- 3 slices of pancetta/streaky bacon

Start the pancetta off in a cold pan and heat gradually. Pour any excess fat off as the pancetta starts to crisp.

Once dark golden, drain on baking paper and allow to cool. Roughly chop into small pieces.

In a bowl mix the olive oil and lemon juice and pepper, add the pear and toss well to thoroughly coat the pear slices [this will stop them from browning]. Add the spinach and grapes and toss. Lastly add the nuts, cheese and pancetta to the top of the salad. Don't toss until just ready to serve.

LUXURY COLESLAW

- 2 large carrots
- 2 large parsnips small red cabbage
- large piece of butternut squash
- 4 small red radishes
- juice and zest of 2 lemons
- 200ml of crème fraiche
- 200ml greek yoghurt
- salt and pepper to taste

Either on a mandolin or with a sharp knife carefully slice the peeled vegetables into rough matchstick size pieces, and the radishes into thin rounds.

In a large bowl mix the crème fraiche and yoghurt with the lemon juice, add the vegetables and season to taste.

Soups

TOMATO & RED PEPPER SOUP

- 2 shallots or 1 red onion
- 2 red peppers
- 2 garlic cloves
- 1 mild chilli pepper
- 6 large tomatoes
- 2 sticks of celery, leaves and all
- large handful each of – parsley and basil
- juice and zest of 1 lemon
- 60ml olive oil
- 2 big glugs of sherry vinegar
- small pinch sugar or squeeze of honey
- big pinch of sea salt
- generous grinding of black pepper

Peel and roughly chop the vegetables and herbs and put them into a blender. Add the rest of the ingredients and blitz until as smooth as you would like. Add a little water if soup seems too thick.

This 'no cooking required' recipe is very healthy. Full of Vitamin C it will help boost your immune system in the summer months ready for winter.

COURGETTE & LEMON SOUP

- courgettes/zucchini
- 1 garlic clove
- handful of basil
- 3 very ripe lemons
- 200ml of crème fraiche or Greek yoghurt
- 400ml of chilled chicken stock

Roughly chop the courgettes and put them into a blender.

Add the chicken stock and garlic and blend until rough. Add the basil and blend until smooth. Stir in the crème fraiche or yoghurt, lemon juice and zest and season to taste.

CARROT, CORIANDER AND CHILLI SOUP

- 15 large carrots
- 3 sticks of celery
- 1 apple
- 1 lime
- 2 bunches of coriander, finely chopped
- 1 or 2 chillies (depending on the heat), finely chopped
- salt and pepper

Using a juicing machine; roughly chop the carrots, celery and apple and put them through the juicer. Add the coriander and chilli, lime juice and season to taste.

Sauces

CHILLI SAUCE FOR STEAKS

- 3 chillies
- 2 garlic cloves
- bunch of parsley
- 1 tbs of tarragon chopped
- 2 tbs mint, chopped
- 2 tbs coriander, chopped
- 2 tbs olive oil
- 1 tbs Worcestershire sauce
- 1 tsp Tabasco

Place all the ingredients into a blender and whizz until roughly chopped into small pieces. Season to taste. Serve cold on the side

MINTY PASTE FOR BBQ LAMB

- 1 large bunch each of mint and basil, finely chopped
- 4 spring onions, sliced
- 2 tbs crème fraiche
- 2 tbs lime juice
- salt and pepper

Mix all the ingredients together just before serving cold with hot roast lamb.

Mint

Chives

Basil

Thyme

Parsley

Rosemary

Which herb to use?

A simple herb salad, bulked up with tasty baby greens is a great accompaniment to so many summer dishes, especially when the BBQ is in use. This can add a new dimension to grilled meats and fish.

Chicken	basil, thyme, lemon thyme, oregano, marjoram, coriander
Beef	Tarragon, parsley, coriander, chives, garlic chives
Lamb	Mint, coriander, chives, spring onions, parsley
Fish/seafood	dill, parsley, coriander, chives

Remember gently but thoroughly wash the herbs in slightly salted iced water, and allow to dry on kitchen paper.

Always dress the herbs and leaves with a little vinaigrette. Roughly 1 part acid: 3 part oil. E.g. lemon juice and olive oil with a pinch of sugar. Then season with a little sea salt and cracked black pepper.

Abundance

TOO MUCH AT A TIME!

Your growing efforts will at some times in the season produce a glut. Everyone has their own preferences for what to do with excess – here are some of ours.

Freeze herbs as they grow

Parsley and Coriander

- crop them as they grow
- wash well, dry and chop
- freeze in small containers

Their colour and flavour will not change. Use them later in the year in stir fry, sauces and soups.
Just break out what you need – when you need it!

Dry and Store

Chilli peppers are easily dried, crumbled and stored in small containers.

Mint, Oregano and **Thyme** – either as for chillies or dry in bunches and break off what you need – when you need it.

Store in Oil

Garlic

- We grow our year's supply of garlic over the winter when many other crops won't grow.
- Bunches of garlic drying can look pretty.
- Peel enough at a time to fill a jar –a Kilner jar is good but any jar with a tight lid will be fine.

- Cover with olive oil. Keep in the fridge.
- When you need a few cloves – scoop them out. The oil takes on the flavour of the garlic and makes great garlic bread.

Chillies

- The same as garlic
- Use the chillies by scooping out or use the chilli flavoured oil.

Green Salad leaves

- No matter how good you are at sowing at intervals – at some time there are always more salad leaves than you can use.
- Don't let them go to waste!
- In small containers, puree and freeze as a base for a green soup.

Basil

- Make into a pesto. Freeze and enjoy with pasta.

Tomatoes

- Make passata
- Try different sauces –
  tomato, garlic and basil
  tomato, onion and mushroom
  tomato and basil
  Endless combinations

Fruit

The produce of your fruit bushes and trees give loads of options.
Flans, pies, tarts, jams, jellies, pureed sauces, smoothies

New recipes

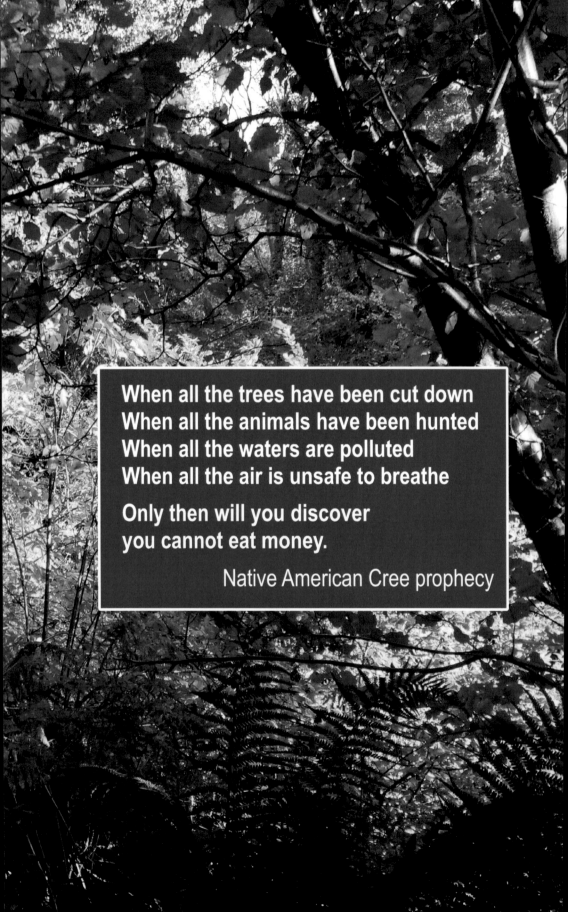

When all the trees have been cut down
When all the animals have been hunted
When all the waters are polluted
When all the air is unsafe to breathe

Only then will you discover
you cannot eat money.

Native American Cree prophecy

Localise

Start a sustainable Community Market Garden Enterprise Network

Extensive flooding in some countries, lengthy droughts in others, temperature extremes - our climatic patterns worldwide are changing in recent times.

Weather extremes have resulted in widespread crop failures.

The global, commercial, economic and financial systems fluctuation has had a disastrous effect on communities across the continents.

However it is the extent to which our food production depends on fossil fuel and its derivatives that is inexorably driving up the price of our food.

Countries can be major exporters of food yet they have millions of people starving or in food poverty [i.e. there is food available but they cannot afford to buy it].

There is an obvious solution.

Localise to recession-proof your community.

If a community has a **localised social economy** - local produce, local retail, local jobs - the products they require are made . . .

- **FOR** the community,
- **IN** the community,
- **BY** the community,
- **TO THE BENEFIT** of the community –
  such a community will have a **robust, stable and sustainable future.**

Of all the possible enterprises which meet the needs of a community, **food production and processing** is the most basic. Everyone needs to eat!

With the Green-way food production system, as described in this book, the start-up capital requirement is low.

Selling locally = minimum number of food miles involved

Selling direct to the consumer = all the money goes to the grower/producer

The customer will get better, fresher, tastier and more nutritious food at a lower cost than with the current, mostly supermarket-based retail chain. The grower/producer will always get a good price. Long term – job opportunities will result. Supply your premier produce directly to the chefs in your local cafes, restaurants and hotels and the business model also embraces your **local green leisure and tourism sector.**

Everyone wins.

Localised thinking

If all the money we earn as a community remains in the community, it will generate a robust and sustainable local production and retail sector. Many local jobs will be created and the community will have environmental, economic and social benefits. Your community will become more vibrant and cohesive – as well as healthier. If businesses are not-for-profit social enterprises, the money in a community just keeps circulating. **Easy!**

Localised Enterprise

The Green-way – as a business model has low capital start-up costs and few energy costs. It has no fertiliser or pesticide costs. Running costs are largely for labour – job creating.

Traditionally, the weaknesses of a market garden business are its seasonality. This can be countered, and value added to the produce, by diversifying into making preserves. This absorbs the seasonal gluts of excess production and gives a product line with a long shelf life – jams, chutneys, relish, preserves, sauces etc. All Organic, tasty and nutritious – and offering a further employment strand.

Community Supported Agriculture [CSA].

Traditionally the farmer is at the start of a very long retail chain. All too often, only a small percentage of the product price in the supermarket goes to the hard working farmer. He is exposed to market fluctuations which he cannot influence. Farming can be a very high risk business. His fuel, fertilisers and pesticides costs are high and increasing constantly.

A community requires certain crops in quantity – potatoes, carrots, onions, turnip etc. these need to be produced on a farm scale – along with the milk, butter, cheese, eggs, meat and meat products.

Grown Organically – without fertilisers, pesticides and with consequently reduced fuel costs, community Organic farming offers a robust and sustainable business model.

With the Green-way, by buying direct from the grower, any community can have food and economic security.

It is a tool against **food poverty** and for vibrant,
healthy sustainable communities for the future.

SEER Rockdust

[Organically approved], has proven to be most effective in mineral replacement. It is a freshly crushed, finely ground basalt dust which contains all minerals and trace elements essential for healthy soil and therefore healthy plants. It helps the soil to absorb carbon from the atmosphere.

As explained on Page 47, you can add Rockdust in various ways - to your soil, HotBox and WormBox. This gives exceptional plant vigour and flavour – and our best contribution to the health of our families / communities.

www.binnsoilnutrients.com
ECO INNOVATION IN TAYSIDE

For commercial catering establishments, the Big Hanna Food Composters have been found to be entirely reliable. There are units to suit anything from 75 – 1200 kg of food waste per week.

They are easy to operate and have very low running costs.

www.bighanna.com